Characteristics of Love

Thomas Couch

The Spotted Feather, an imprint of Colorful Crow

Publishing

Published by

The Spotted Feather, an imprint of Colorful Crow Publishing

96 Craig Street Suite112-304 Ellijay, Georgia

http://www.colorfulcrowpublishing.com

ISBN 978-1-964271-09-5 (PB)

ISBN 978-1-964271-10-1 (eB)

Colorful Crow is committed to publishing works of quality and integrity. In that spirit, we are proud to offer this book to our readers; however, the story, the experiences, and the words are the author's alone.

Contents

I dedicate this book to the readers, my Precious Mother and all of my family. And with all due gratitude, I would like to dedicate it to every person that is involved in the ministries worldwide. For their hard work, dedication and love and kindness to all of those who sought the LORD, and found HIM as a result of the many great ministries out there.

May GOD bless you all beyond measure.

And I would especially like to dedicate this book to my sweet wife Helen, one of my biggest supporters.

Sincerely In Christ,

Evangelist

Thomas Couch

REVIVE - ALL MINISTRIES

ISAIAH 57:15

Introduction

I say to you it is a great honor to be the vessel that GOD has used to bring you this book, Characteristics of Love. It is my hope and prayers that GOD will use it to bless you with, just as much as it blessed me to write it. It is also my hope and prayers that you will find something somewhere in this book, that will be an encouragement to you and that the knowledge GOD has revealed to us in this book will help you somewhere along the way in your Christian journey. When we are born into the family of GOD, HE begins to instill HIS very own characteristics in each and every one of us.

I pray that as you read this book and learn from it that GOD will bless you and impart to you many blessings and the unfailing force of the Characteristics of Love.

Chapter One

The Divine Example of Love

1 st JOHN 4:8

He that loveth not knoweth not God; for God is love.

As we examine the first Characteristic of Love, the Divine example of love, we need to take note of what we discover. Because our studies will show that we are indeed supposed to follow that example that GOD has set for us in the Bible.

You see, the word Christian means to be Christ-like. So to be Christ-like is to be GOD-like.

Look at MATTHEW 1:23, it says:

v. 23, Behold, a Virgin shall be with child, and shall bring forth a Son, and they shall call his name

Emmanuel, which being interpreted, is, "God with us".

One of the names the Word of GOD gives Jesus is Emmanuel and the Word of GOD also translates the meaning of that name, (GOD with us) is what it means. So, my dear Christian friend, if the word

Christian means to be Christ-like and the Word of GOD specifically says that Christ is "GOD", with us, and that we are to be like him. Then it is very GOD inspiring and Biblical to say that we as Christians are to be "GOD-like".

Let's look at a divine example of love in action. Remember now, we are to follow these examples in our everyday lives. Jesus Himself says so in this passage we are about to look at.

Look at JOHN 13:1-17, it says:

v. 1, Now before the feast of the Passover, when Jesus knew that his hour was come, that he should depart out of this world unto the Father, having loved his own which were in the world, he loved them unto the end.

v. 2, And Supper being ended, the devil having now put into the heart of Judas Iscariot, Simon's son, to betray him;

v. 3, Jesus knowing that the Father had given all things into his hands, and that he was come from God, and went to God;

v. 4, He riseth from supper, and laid aside his garments; and took a towel, and girded himself.

v. 5, After that he poureth water into a bason, and began to wash the disciples feet, and to wipe them with the towel wherewith he was girded.

v. 6, Then cometh he to Simon Peter: and Peter saith unto him, Lord, dost thou wash my feet?

v. 7, Jesus answered and said unto him, what I do thou knowest not now; but thou shalt know hereafter.

v. 8, Peter saith unto him, Thou shalt never wash my feet. Jesus answered him, If I wash thee not, thou hast no part with me.

v. 9, Simon Peter saith unto him, Lord, not my feet only, but, also my hands and my head.

v. 10, Jesus saith to him, He that is washed needeth not save to wash his feet, but is clean every whit: and ye are clean, but not all.

v. 11, For he knew who should betray him; therefore said he, ye are not all clean.

v. 12, So after he had washed their feet, and had taken his garments, and was set down again, he said unto them, know ye not what I have done to you?

v. 13, Ye call me master and Lord: and ye say well; for so I am.

v. 14, If I then, your Lord and Master, have washed your feet; ye also ought to wash one another's feet.

v. 15, For I have given you an example, that ye should do as I have done to you.

v. 16, Verily, verily, I say unto you, The servant is not greater than his Lord; neither he that is sent greater than he that sent him.

v. 17, If ye know these things, happy are ye if ye do them.

Dear Christian friend, this passage may indeed be symbolic of cleansing one another from our ugly pasts. However, the action of doing it in our everyday lives is a powerful act of love. Jesus is showing us what HE did for us, in HIS redemptive work on the Cross. The ultimate act of love, in which HE cleansed all of our past's.

Now, look at what HE, Jesus, says in verse 15, it says:

v. 15, For I have given you an example, that ye should do as I have done to you.

The first Characteristic of Love that I am going to give you is, The Divine example of love. The example is a Characteristic of Love that you must follow. This is a command that Jesus is giving you and I. HE is telling us in verse 15 to follow HIS example.

Jesus is also telling us in this passage that we are to put it into action. When we put love into action, that is, when we will find true happiness.

Look again at what Jesus said in verse 17, it says:

v. 17, If ye know these things, happy are ye if ye do them.

So HE is telling us to use the wisdom HE has given us. HE said, If ye know these things, (once we learn them) we are then to apply them and take action. HE said if you know them, happy are ye if ye do them. Praise GOD!

My dear Christian friend, I can tell you from my own personal experience that when you learn the Word of GOD and then you start applying it to your every day lives, you will indeed be happy and blessed. Jesus said it!

That is why the Bible says for us to study, to show ourselves approved to GOD. Let's look at the Scripture, it is 2nd TIMOTHY 2:15, it says:

v. 15, Study to shew thyself approved unto God, a workman that needeth not to be ashamed, rightly dividing the word of truth. This verse tells us basically the same thing Jesus said. First, we study the Word of GOD. We learn it, we learn what it tells us to do, and we learn the examples it shows us to do. Then we apply that to our lives and we show GOD, not man, but GOD, that we are diligently seeking HIM and to be like HIM.

Dear Christian friend, you and I "must" learn to rightly divide the word of truth so that we can "rightly apply" it to our lives. Let me show you an ultimate example of wrongly and rightly dividing and applying the word of truth. Look at MATTHEW 4:1-10, it says:

v. 1, Then was Jesus led up of the Spirit into the wilderness to be tempted of the devil.

v. 2, And when he had fasted forty days and forty nights, he was afterward and hungred.

v. 3, And when the tempter came to him, he said, If thou be the Son of God, Command that these stones be made bread.

v. 4, But he answered and said, It is written, Man shall not live by bread alone, but by every word that proceedeth out of the mouth of God.

v. 5, Then the devil taketh him up into the holy city, and setteth him on a pinnacle of the temple.

v. 6, And saith unto him, If thou be the Son of God, cast thyself down: for it is written, He shall give his angels charge concerning thee: and in their hands they shall bear thee up, lest at anytime thou dash thy foot against a stone.

v. 7, Jesus said unto him, It is written again, thou shalt not tempt the Lord thy God.

v. 8, Again, the devil taketh him up into an exceeding high mountain, and sheweth him all the Kingdoms of the world, and the glory of them;

v. 9, And saith unto him, All these things will I give thee, if thou wilt fall down and worship me.

v. 10, Then saith Jesus unto him, Get thee hence, Satan: for it is written, Thou shalt worship the Lord thy God, and him only shalt thou serve.

Now dear Christian, pay close attention to this because if you are a born again Christian, you will one day experience this from the devil. In this passage, we see Satan both wrongly dividing the word of truth and trying to get Jesus to wrongly "apply" the word of truth. The devil tried to get Jesus to kill Himself and he used GOD'S Word in a very wrong way to persuade Jesus to do it. Notice each time Satan would wrongly divide the Word and tempt Jesus to wrongly apply it, Jesus would turn around and rightly divide it and rightly apply it.

There is a world full of people today, even some Christians that Satan has tricked into wrongly dividing and wrongly applying GOD'S Word. Let me give you an example. A lot of people will take the verse out of MATTHEW to defend a destructive smoking addiction, look at this verse, MATTHEW 15:11, it says:

v. 11, Not that which goeth into the mouth defileth a man, but that which cometh out of the mouth, this defileth a man.

Satan has deceived them into slowly killing themselves by tricking them into wrongly applying that verse. They say it's not what goes in the mouth that defiles a man, it's what comes out. So in their deception, they think it is o.k. to smoke according to that verse. That is wrongly dividing and wrongly applying GOD'S Word.

What they need to do is look over in 1st CORINTHIANS 3:16-17. It says:

v. 16, Know ye not that ye are the temple of God, and that the Spirit of God dwelleth in you?

v. 17, If any man defile the temple of God, him shall God destroy; for the temple of God is holy, which temple ye are.

So dear Christians, we should rightly divide this verse and say to the devil, my body is the temple of the Holy Spirit and then rightly apply it to that situation, and say it is written. GOD dwelleth in my body and my body belongs to GOD. So I am not going to put anymore of that Poison in my body, no more smoking, no more drugs, no more alcohol, It is written my body is GOD'S temple.

However, I don't believe that smoking and drinking is a sin, because the Word of GOD says to drink moderately. I don't think it will keep you from going to Heaven, but it might get you there a lot faster.

"That", my dear Christian friend, is how we rightly divide and rightly apply GOD'S Word!

This Chapter is on The Divine Example of Love. A Characteristic that we need to know. Jesus sets many divine examples for us to follow.

Let's look at another example the Word of GOD gives us on loving one another. Look at 1st JOHN 4:11 and 17, it says:

v. 11, Beloved, if God so loved us, we ought also to love one another.

v. 17, Herein is our love made perfect, that we may have boldness in the day of judgment: because as he is, so are we in this world.

Praise GOD!

Dear Christians, the Bible is full of divine examples of love. The example is a Characteristic that we have to rightly apply to have perfect love. Verse 11 here says very clearly, follow GOD'S example, it says, Beloved, if God so loved us, we ought to also love one another. That is very vividly telling us to follow GOD'S Divine Example of Love. It tells us GOD loved us, so we ought to love one another, follow GOD'S example.

Then verse 17 says, Herein is our love made perfect, in the first half of the verse, then the last half says, because as he, (God) is, so are we in this world. Praise GOD friend, this is another very clear example, it says; "as he is," so are we in this world. This verse gives a very vivid divine example of love for us to follow. As he is, so are we in this world.

Glory to GOD!

Dear Christians, listen to me closely now, you and I are supposed to be an example of The Divine example maker. We are to follow

GOD'S example of being an example. The first and most valuable Characteristic of Love, is indeed The Divine Example of Love. Glory to GOD!

Chapter Two

The Walk of Love

E PHESIANS 5:2
And walk in love, as Christ also hath loved us, and hath given himself for us an offering and a sacrifice to God for a sweet smelling savour.

Fellow Christians, the walk of love is the second Characteristic of Love that I will ask you to look at with me. What this is saying here is, love has a walk. In other words, love has a conduct. A certain way that you must live to practice love.

This verse goes right back to what I was telling you in the first chapter about following divine examples. Look at it, it says, walk in love, "as" Christ also has loved us. It also goes back to studying the word, finding the examples and applying them to our lives. Walking in them in other words.

Let's look at some ways that we are to walk or present ourselves in love. Look at EPHESIANS 5:25, it says:

v. 25, Husbands, love your wives, even as Christ also loved the Church, and gave himself for it;

Glory to GOD Christians, we men are to love our wives, even as Christ also loved the Church. Let me explain something here, this verse also applies to the women. Both men and women are to love one another, Husband and wife that is, as Christ also loved the Church.

You may say, well, how did Christ love the Church? This verse right here tells us, HE gave Himself for it. Jesus gave "everything" for the Church. Even HIS very life, right down to the precious blood that flowed through HIS body.

Please allow me to show you a few more verses that show very clearly that love has a conduct.

Look at 1st CORINTHIANS 13:4-7, it says:

v. 4, Charity suffereth long, and is kind; Charity envieth not; Charity vaunteth not itself, is not puffed up.

v. 5, Doth not behave itself unseemly, seeketh not her own, is not easily provoked, thinketh no evil;

v. 6, Rejoiceth not in iniquity, but rejoiceth in the truth;

v. 7, Beareth all things, believeth all things, hopeth all things, endureth all things.

This word Charity, is in the Greek "Agape", which actually means love. And it is the kind of love that we have to ask GOD to teach us how to live.

Glory to GOD!

Look at some of the things that we can see love doing. The first thing we see is that the GOD kind of love that you and I are desiring to experience is long-suffering. That is Patience. This is the kind of Patience only the Holy Spirit can give us. As a matter of fact, the long-suffering or patience that we are talking about is the fruit of the Spirit.

Let me give you an example of this kind of patience. The kind of patience that only the Spirit of GOD can give you. Look at EXODUS 14:10-13, it says:

v. 10, And when Pharaoh drew nigh, the Children of Israel lifted up their eyes, and behold, the Egyptians marched after them; and they were sore afraid: and the Children of Israel cried out unto the Lord.

v. 11, And they said unto Moses, Because there were no graves in Egypt, hast thou taken us away to die in the wilderness? Wherefore hast thou dealt thus with us, to carry us forth out of Egypt?

v. 12, Is not this the word that we did tell thee in Egypt, saying, Let us alone, that we may serve the Egyptians? For it had been better for us to serve the Egyptians, than that we should die in the wilderness.

v. 13, And Moses said unto the people, Fear ye not, stand still and see the Salvation of the Lord, which he will shew to you today: for the Egyptians whom ye have seen today, ye shall see them again no more forever.

Now, dear Christian People, let me show you an awesome display of the GOD kind of Patience our love should express. Check this out. Pharaoh and his army was closing in on these people. Verse 10 says that the Egyptians marched after them. They had already gotten so close to them, they stopped running and started marching. They were probably in ranks and sounding off. They were not just running up on them, this time they were there and they were making a military advance, moving in for the kill.

The Children of Israel just knew they were dead meat this time. Look at verse 11, they were already looking for a grave to bury themselves in. They said there were no graves in Egypt, now we are going to die in the wilderness. Listen, GOD was giving them Patience right then, and they did not even realize it. They were standing there talking about getting killed when they could have been running or swimming or fighting for their lives.

Praise GOD Christians!

Now, look at what Moses said to them in verse 13, He said "Stand Still" and see the Salvation of the Lord. I can just picture these people just standing there, finally in a situation where all that they could do was trust in GOD. They could have been jumping in the water or running down the seaside to the left or right and Moses was telling them to "Stand Still". They probably looked at one another like, o.k. you let me lean on your shoulder and pick my teeth until they kill me, and I will leave you my toothpick. They were ready to die and Moses said, "have Patience".

Dear Christians, only GOD can give us that kind of Patience. We, in our human nature, cannot produce such divine Patience. If you will read on in that Passage, you will see the results. GOD destroyed the whole Egyptian army and the Children of Israel lived to make more toothpicks.

My point is, love has Patience, no matter what we are facing, the Holy Spirit will give us the Patience to stand still until we get the victory. True "Agape" love will wait Patiently for a desired result and Praise GOD, the result that you desire will come. GOD will give you the Patience to wait for it.

Another aspect of love's walk - Conduct is kindness. This is also fruit of the Holy Spirit, it falls under "Goodness". Just like I took you to the Passage in EXODUS and showed you how the Holy Spirit gave the people Patience while standing there thinking they were going to die. HE could have also have given them kindness in the face of death.

Dear fellow Christians, the Holy Spirit will help you and I to practice this kind of loving behavior, so that HE can shine forth HIS divine "Agape" love through us.

Another aspect of the Conduct of love, is that it envieth not. Do you know why love does not envy? It is because, to envy, is to covet. And GOD'S Word tells us not to covet.

Another aspect of love's Conduct is that it "vaunteth not itself". To Vaunt is to boast, and again that is something that GOD'S Word tells us not to do. So if we are to walk in real "Agape" love, it has to be in line with GOD'S Word. GOD is not going to have us doing anything that is contrary to HIS word. That goes back to rightly dividing and rightly applying GOD'S Word. It is all a matter of how we "apply" the Word of GOD to our lives.

Another aspect of love is, it is not puffed up. In other words, it is not proud. The Bible also has something to say about Pride. Look at PROVERBS 16:18, it says:

v. 18, Pride goeth before destruction, and a haughty Spirit before a fall.

So you see, if we are sincerely walking in true GOD-like love, then we are not going to be puffed up. Do you remember what John the Baptist said? He said that he had to decrease so that Jesus could be increased. That is how we must be and the Holy Spirit will enable us to do it.

The next aspect of love is, it does not behave itself unseemingly. That means it does not behave improper. So then, if there is an improper way that love does not behave like, then Glory to GOD, there is a proper way. GOD'S Word, the Bible, is what shows us the proper way to love and thank GOD the Holy Spirit helps us to love one another in a seemingly GOD-like manner.

This Passage also says that love seeketh not her own. That is true "Agape", GOD-like love is unselfish. It always puts others first. We "have" to have the help of the Holy Spirit to function like this dear people of GOD. We cannot do it on our own. But Praise GOD, the Holy Spirit will help us to be like John the Baptist and humbly step aside, so that the love of Jesus will increase in our every day lives.

True GOD-like "Agape" love is not easily provoked. You look back through the Old Testament at how the people repeatedly sinned and just openly disobeyed GOD. Yet GOD, in HIS awesome love, would not let them provoke HIM to completely do them in. HE could have ended human existence thousands of years ago. Thank GOD that sincere love is not easily provoked. Love thinketh no evil. The Bible shows us from GENESIS to REVELATION that GOD has always thought good for us. HE wants to bless us in every area of our lives. GOD-like love does not think evil or have any evil intentions. GOD-like love does not rejoice in iniquity, but it does rejoice in truth. GOD'S Word, and Jesus is the truth, and they set the example of true GOD-like "Agape" love. The kind that you and I long to walk in, and that the Precious Holy Spirit will enable us to experience. True love beareth all things, believeth all things, hopeth all things, endureth all things.

My Dear Christian Friends, the Bible clearly tells us to walk in love. And we have seen that love has a conduct. We have also just seen that GOD commands us to love the way HE loves, and that we must keep our love standards in line with GOD'S Word and ways. GOD tells us to do it, HE shows us how to do it, and Praise GOD, HE gave us the Holy Spirit to enable us to do it. So I encourage you, my Dear Christian Friend, to walk in love, behave in love, and Conduct your life in love.

The Second Characteristic of Love is "The Walk Of Love". Glory to GOD!

Chapter Three

The Courage of Love

J OSHUA 1:9

    Have not I commanded thee? Be strong and of good courage; be not afraid, neither be thou dismayed: for the Lord thy God is with thee whithersoever thou goest.

    Fellow Christians, the third Characteristic of Love that I am going to give you is the Courage of Love. Before we go any further into our study, let me show you how very important this Characteristic is.

    Look at REVELATION 21:8, it says:

    v. 8, But the "fearful", and unbelieving, and the abominable, and murderers, and whoremongers, and sorcerers, and idolaters, and all liars, shall have their part in the lake which burneth with fire and brimstone: which is the second death.

    The first person this verse names is the fearful. So without courage, the third Characteristic of Love, a person cannot even go to Heaven. That is how very important this characteristic is.

Let's look at our opening verse on this subject. JOSHUA 1:9, it says:

v. 9, Have not I commanded thee? Be strong and of a good courage; be not afraid, neither be thou dismayed: for the Lord thy God is with thee whithersoever thou goest.

So we can see here that GOD has commanded us to have Courage. Let me tell you something dear Christian friend, when GOD commands us to do something, it is always for a very important reason. Here in this verse, the last part of it says, "for the Lord thy God is with thee whithersoever thou goest". So we can see that GOD is commanding us to have Courage because HE is right there with us wherever we go. I can tell you it is much easier to overcome fear and have Courage when you know without a doubt that GOD is with you. When you do not know for sure that GOD is with you, is when you start getting fearful; and when you are fearful, you cannot fully function in love.

Let's look at a verse that will prove my point on this issue. Look at 1st JOHN 4:18, it says:

v. 18, There is no fear in love, but perfect love casteth out fear: because fear hath torment. He that feareth is not made perfect in love.

The Greek word for fear in this passage is "Phobos" and it is where we get our English word Phobia. Now Phobia is an over-powering fear and it causes mental torment. Not only that, but it will also hinder your Spiritual growth. It will also prevent you from becoming perfect in love. In other words, you will not be able to function in love the way that you want to, if you are fearful.

I must confess, I was one of the world's worst about being fearful of what could happen. If I was afraid something might happen, I would focus all of my attention and strength on that Phobia and take my eyes off of GOD.

"Now", I have my favorite verse that I stand on to help me be courageous. It is ROMANS 8:28, it says:

v. 28, And we know that all things work together for good to them that love God, to them who are the called according to his purpose.

GOD gave me this verse after a very fearful event. Once I realized that the event was just a little trial, and that after it was over, I had conquered that fear. I could then see that even the little trials that we face will work together for our good. Mine helped me overcome that fear, which in turn helped me grow Spiritually, which helped me draw closer to GOD and acknowledge HIM more in my life, which will ultimately help me be perfected in love, and be able to function in the GOD-like "Agape" love that we all want to experience in our every day lives. So you see, GOD commands us to have courage for our own good.

Again, this type of courage comes only from the Holy Spirit. And I can tell you from personal experience, that if you stay a Christian long enough, GOD is going to teach you how to have courage. HE will also take you through something to help you overcome fear and establish courage in your life. HE did it with me, and I will show you a very popular passage in the Bible where GOD took someone through an awesome adventure to help them have courage. Let's look at it; JONAH Chapter One, it says:

v. 1, Now the word of the Lord came unto Jonah, the son of Amittai saying,

v. 2, Arise, go to Nineveh, that great City, and cry against it; for their wickedness is come up before me.

v. 3, But Jonah rose up to flee unto Tarshish from the Presence of the Lord, and went down to Joppa; and he found a ship going to Tarshish: so he paid the fair thereof, and went down into it, to go with them unto Tarshish from the Presence of the Lord.

v. 4, But the Lord sent out a great wind into the sea, and there was a mighty tempest in the sea, so that the ship was like to be broken.

v. 5, Then the mariners were afraid, and cried every man unto his god, and cast forth the wares that were in the ship into the sea, to lighten it of them. But Jonah was gone down into the sides of the ship, and he lay, and was fast asleep.

v. 6, So the shipmaster came to him, and said unto him, what meanest thou, O sleeper? Arise, call upon thy God, if so be that God will think upon us, that we perish not.

v. 7, And they said every one to his fellow, come, and let us cast lots, that we may know for whose cause this evil is upon us. So they cast lots, and the lot fell upon Jonah.

v. 8, Then said they unto him, tell us, we pray thee, for whose cause this evil is upon us; what is thine occupation? and whence comest thou? What is thy Country? and of what people art thou?

v. 9, And he said unto them, I am an Hebrew; and I fear the Lord, the God of heaven, which hath made the sea and the dry land.

v. 10, Then were the men exceedingly afraid, and said unto him, why hast thou done this? For the men knew that he fled from the presence of the Lord, because he had told them.

v. 11, Then said they unto him, what shall we do unto thee: that the sea may be calm unto us? For the sea wrought, and was tempestuous.

v. 12, And he said unto them, Take me up, and cast me forth into the sea; so shall the sea be calm unto you: for I know that for my sake this great tempest is upon you.

v. 13, Nevertheless the men rowed hard to bring it to the land; but they could not: for the sea wrought, and was tempestuous against them.

v. 14, Wherefore they cried unto the Lord, and said, we beseech thee, O Lord, we beseech thee, let us not perish for this man's life, and lay not upon us innocent blood: for thou, O Lord, hast done as it pleased thee.

v. 15, So they took up Jonah, and cast him forth into the sea: and the sea ceased from her raging.

v. 16, Then the men feared the Lord exceedingly, and offered a sacrifice unto the Lord, and made vows.

v. 17, Now, the Lord had prepared a great fish to swallow up Jonah. And Jonah was in the belly of the fish three days and three nights.

Praise GOD Christians!

Here we see a man of GOD who is fearful. Jonah was afraid to go and cry out against the people of Nineveh. They were wicked people. GOD said so in verse two, GOD said their wickedness has come up before me.

Look at verse three, it says: Jonah rose up to "flee". Jonah did fear GOD, but he also feared what would happen if he went out there crying out against those wicked people. So he tried to run. GOD knew that Jonah did not have the courage to go, so GOD made all of these things happen to help Jonah establish the courage that he needed to do GOD'S will. Look at verse four, it says: "the Lord" sent out a great wind into the sea. Praise GOD People! GOD created the storm in Jonah's life to build up his courage. Jonah was afraid they would kill him, so GOD took him to a near death experience and showed him that HE could deliver him from even death. GOD made Jonah face his fear of dying. Jonah thought for sure that he was going to die when those men threw him overboard into the raging waters. He knew that GOD was after him, and that if he did not do something, those men were going to be destroyed because of him. So he faced his fear of death, and he told them in verse twelve to cast him into the sea and the storm would stop. Jonah faced his fear of death, and he was ready to die.

Although Jonah was ready to die, he was just about to learn how to live. "For GOD!" The storm had settled when Jonah hit the water, and he probably thought the water was calm enough to swim the distance. However, verse seventeen says, that GOD prepared another near death experience by sending a great fish to swallow him up. My GOD, that is awesome. You know, Jonah must have thought for sure that he was a dead man when that fish swallowed him up. But GOD spoke to the fish and told it to spit Jonah out.

Dear Christian, I can assure you that if GOD drives you to face your fears like HE did Jonah, you will indeed be ready to do whatever GOD has for you to do. And you will do it boldly with the courage that the Holy Spirit will give you. And Praise GOD when you do it, you will succeed just like Jonah did. After he preached to Nineveh, they repented and got it right.

Glory to GOD!

You may say, GOD is not going to do anybody like that. Oh yes HE will! Can the Clay say to the Potter why are you making me this way? GOD will do whatever it takes to help us live the way that HE wants us to. It may be a fearful experience, and you may pass through some pretty rough waters, but, I assure you when the storm is over and you experience the reward of riding the storm out, you will lift up your voice and thank GOD for it. Jonah thanked GOD when he realized what GOD was doing. Look at Jonah 2:9, it says:

v. 9, But I will sacrifice unto thee with the voice of thanksgiving; I will pay that that I have vowed.

Salvation is of the Lord.

Jonah was still in the fish's belly when he started thanking GOD. "You", my dear friend, will do the very same thing when you realize that whatever you go through could be used by GOD to produce something in your life. So then fearless Christians, when fear starts to rise up in your life; whatever the case may be, you stand up boldly and apply the third Characteristic of Love - The Courage of Love, and speak PSALMS 118:6 to it, it says:

v. 6, The Lord is on my side; I will not fear: what can man do unto me?

Speak to that fear in the name of Jesus and tell it that it is written in PSALMS 118:6, you will not fear! Praise GOD, then stand boldly in that third Characteristic of Love, and watch the victory surface in that situation.

Love has Courage!

Chapter Four

The Royal Law of Love

JAMES 2:8

J   If ye fulfil the royal law according to the Scripture, Thou shalt love thy neighbor as thyself, ye do well.

People of GOD, the fourth Characteristic of Love that I want us to look at is "The Royal Law of Love". We have seen that love has examples, it has a walk - conduct, it has courage, and Praise GOD love has a royal law to abide by. Unlike the law of the Old Testament that we could not keep, this law of love is one that, through GOD'S grace and the power of the Holy Spirit we can keep.

Look at JAMES 2:8, it says:

v. 8, If ye fulfil the royal law according to the Scripture, Thou shalt love thy neighbor as thyself, ye do well.

This verse says, "if" you (fulfil) the royal law, so this law of love can be fulfilled, dear people. You may say how in the world can we fulfil that law of love? Actually, this same verse also tells us how to fulfil the royal law of love. It says "according to Scripture", you have to study the Scripture and prayerfully ask GOD to help you fulfil the royal law of love. You look at HIS examples, you look at HIS conduct, you look at HIS courage, and you prayerfully apply all of these Characteristics of Love to your personal life. Then dear Christians, you begin to fulfil the royal law of love, and look at the last part of this verse, It says: if you do these things and fulfil the royal law of love, "ye do well".

Let's examine another passage that very vividly shows that love has a law to abide by, and that it can be fulfilled. Look at ROMANS 13:8-10, it says:

v. 8, Owe no man anything, but to love one another: for he that loveth another hath fulfilled the law.

v. 9, For this, Thou shalt not commit adultery, thou shalt not kill, thou shalt not steal, thou shalt not bear false witness, thou shalt not covet; and if there be any other commandment, it is briefly comprehended in this saying, namely, Thou shalt love thy neighbor as thyself.

v. 10, Love worketh no ill to his neighbor: therefore love is the fulfilling of the law.

Praise GOD Dear Christians, this passage is not referring to the law of the Old Testament. It is referring to the fourth Characteristic of Love, "The Royal Law Of Love." The one that with GOD'S help, you can fulfil.

Look at what it says in verse 8, it says: for he that "loveth" another hath fulfilled the law. Dear Christians, it is talking about the Royal Law of Love. Then it goes on to say in verse 10, that love worketh no ill to his neighbor. People of GOD, if you are loving somebody, you do not work ill to them. You do not hit them over the head with a ball bat and say I love you.

When you apply GOD'S (Agape) love, it will show. Love itself is fruit of the Spirit, and when love is in action, you will see the rest of the fruit of the Spirit at work. They are Joy, Peace, Long-suffering, Gentleness, Goodness, Faith, Meekness, Temperance. So you see, if you are applying the love that the Spirit of GOD gives you, there is no way you will be committing adultery or killing anyone or stealing or bearing false witness or coveting or breaking any other law. That is what this passage is saying. It is not saying you can keep or fulfill the law of the Old Testament, it is saying you can fulfill the royal law of love, and that when you are doing it, you won't be breaking any of the other laws. "Because", love worketh no ill.

Let's look at some powerful verses that Jesus gave us on this subject. Look at the Sermon on the Mount, MATTHEW 5:21, it says:

v. 21, ye have heard that it was said by them of old time, Thou shalt not kill: and whosoever shall kill shall be in danger of judgment.

People of GOD, like I said earlier, if you are loving someone, you are not going to hit them over the head with a ball bat and say I love you. So if you are truly loving them, you most surely won't be killing them. Look at another verse, 5:27, ye have heard that it was said by them of old time, Thou shalt not commit adultery:

Listen Christians, if you are loving your wife or husband with the love GOD gives you, there is no way you will go out and have an adulterous affair on your spouse. You are going to be too busy loving him or her as Christ loved the Church, to have time to get involved in an adulterous affair. Also, if you are loving other people the way GOD teaches you to love one another, there is "no" way you are going to have an adulterous affair with someone else's spouse. You know it would hurt them. So that goes right back to the verse in ROMANS, love worketh "no ill".

Let's look at another verse from MATTHEW 5:38, it says:

v. 38, ye have heard that it hath been said, An eye for an eye, and a tooth for a tooth.

This is a hard one, but with GOD'S help, you can even love someone who goes as far as knocking out your teeth. If you are really loving the way GOD teaches us to, and someone knocks out your teeth, you are not going to pick them up, give them to that person, and then get a ball bat and knock theirs out so you can have a tooth for a tooth. What good would it do? Neither one of you would be able to even chew a piece of bubble gum with another person's tooth. People of GOD, love works no ill. You cannot say, "well I love my brother Bill, but I just had to knock his teeth out for making me mad. If you are loving people with the fruit of the Spirit kind of love, you are going to want to see them delivered from that behavior, so they won't hurt anyone else or so they won't pick a fight with someone who owns a bigger ball bat than they have.

Let's look at another passage that Jesus gave us in the Sermon on the Mount, it is MATTHEW 5:43-48, it says:

v. 43, ye have heard that it hath been said, Thou shalt love thy neighbor, and hate thine enemy.

v. 44, But I say unto you, Love your enemies, bless them that curse you, do good to them that hate you, and pray for them which despitefully use you, and persecute you;

v. 45, That ye may be the Children of your Father which is in heaven: for he maketh his sun to rise on the evil and on the good, and he sendeth rain on the just, and the unjust.

v. 46, For if ye love them which love you, what reward have ye? Do not even the Publicans the same?

v. 47, And if ye salute your brethren only, what do ye more than others? Do not even the Publicans so?

v. 48, Be ye therefore perfect, even as your Father which is in heaven is perfect.

Precious People of GOD, what Jesus is telling us in this passage is to love everybody unconditionally. Even in the face of evil hatred, love that person. Even in the face of wicked spitefulness, love that person. Even in the face of inconsiderate evil cursing, love that person. Even in the face of someone despitefully using you, love that person. Even in the face of somebody evilly persecuting you, love that person. You see, Jesus knew how to fulfill the royal law of love. Jesus knew the Scriptures, Jesus knew how to apply PROVERBS 15:1-2, it says:

v. 1, A soft answer turneth away wrath: but grievous words stir up anger.

v. 2, The tongue of the wise useth knowledge aright: but the mouth of fools poureth out foolishness.

Jesus knew that in the face of any situation, if we just speak soft, loving words to that person, it would turn away wrath. That is what verse 2 is saying, the tongue of the wise useth knowledge aright. If you are wise, you have wisdom. Wisdom is actually successfully applying the knowledge of GOD'S Word to your life. No matter what the situation is, if you will wisely use the knowledge that you have of GOD'S Word "aright" you will have the victory over that situation. And if you love everyone with the fruit of the Spirit kind of love, that is rightly applying the fourth Characteristic of Love to your life.

Fellow Christians, when we apply GOD'S Word to our life like this, we are actually obeying GOD'S commandments. When we start obeying GOD'S Word, HE will bless us. In this same passage where

Jesus is telling us to love everybody, he said, "for he (GOD) maketh his sun to rise on the evil and on the good, and sendeth rain on the just and the unjust. So what this is saying is, that GOD will bless you for doing good and for being just. It is also saying that GOD will chastise you for being evil and unjust.

You see, if you are out fishing or swimming, or flying a kite, you are going to want the sun to be shining brightly and the wind to be just right. Dear Christian, if you have a garden, there is going to be certain times you are going to need the sun to shine, and there is going to be certain times you are going to need the rain to fall on that garden to bless it and make it grow.

I can tell you this Precious people of GOD, If you are doing good and just things for GOD, and you are fulfilling the royal law of love, GOD will make the sun shine brightly just when you need it to, and HE will make the rain fall sweetly on your garden just when you need rain. HE will send an awesome blessing your way just when you need an awesome blessing. Keep in mind also, that if you are being evil and unjust, GOD will send the rain when you want sunshine and sunshine when you want rain.

Fellow Christians, I have showed you that if you are fulfilling the royal law of love, that you won't be breaking any of the other laws. The golden rule is the last verse I will give you to help you understand the fourth Characteristic of Love, The Royal Law Of Love. The golden rule is found in MATTHEW 7:12, and it says basically the same thing as JAMES 2:8, let's compare.

MATTHEW 7:12, Therefore all things whatsoever ye would that men should do to you, do ye even so to them: for this is the law and the Prophets.

JAMES 2:8, If ye fulfil the royal law according to the Scripture, Thou shalt love thy neighbour as thyself, ye do well.

So if you do good and just to everyone, and you love the unlovable when you don't feel like loving them, GOD will indeed bless you. You will be successfully fulfilling the fourth Characteristic of Love and GOD will honor it.

Glory to GOD! In all of this we find "The Royal Law Of Love"....

Chapter Five

The Divine Revelation Of Love

1 st CORINTHIANS 13:13

And now abideth faith, hope, Charity, these three; but the greatest of these is Charity.

When GOD spoke to me about writing my first book, Characteristics of Faith, I wrote it and I did it prayerfully asking GOD to give me what HE wanted me to write about. As soon as I finished that book, GOD blessed me and gave me my Evangelist's License. Then as I was reading GOD'S Word, HE spoke to me about love. The opening verse here, 1st CORINTHIANS 13:13 actually uses the word Charity for love, and as I read it, GOD said there is three powerful action words in this verse. They are faith, hope and love; but the greatest is love. Then HE spoke to me and said I want you to write another book, this time about love.

So just as the last time I was quick to say OK I will write a book about love. So I started researching and I found a little about it, but not much. So I started prayerfully brainstorming for what to write and I just went to GOD and said, if you want me to write about love, I need you to show me what love really is. GOD says OK. Study 1st CORINTHIANS Chapter 13, so I did and it says: (Remember Charity is love),

v. 1, Though I speak with the tongues of men and of angels, and have not Charity, I am become as sounding brass, or a tinkling cymbal.

v. 2, And though I have the gift of Prophecy, and understand all mysteries, and all knowledge; and though I have all faith, so that I could remove mountains, and have not Charity, I am nothing.

v. 3, And though I bestow all my goods to feed the poor, and though I give my body to be burned, and have not Charity, it profiteth me nothing.

v. 4, Charity suffereth long, and is kind, Charity envieth not; Charity vaunteth not itself, is not puffed up,

v. 5, Doth not behave itself unseemly, seeketh not her own, is not easily provoked, thinketh no evil;

v. 6, Rejoiceth not in iniquity, but rejoiceth in the truth;

v. 7, Beareth all things, believeth all things, hopeth all things, endureth all things.

v. 8, Charity never faileth: but whether there be Prophecies, they shall fail; whether there be tongues, they shall cease; whether there be knowledge, it shall vanish away.

v. 9, For we know in part, and we Prophesy in part.

v. 10, But when that which is perfect is come, then that which is in part shall be done away.

v. 11, When I was a child, I spake as a child, I understood as a child, I thought as a child: but when I became a man, I put away childish things.

v. 12, For now we see through a glass, darkly; but then face to face: now I know in part; but then shall I know even as also I am known.

v. 13, And now abideth faith, hope, Charity, these three, but the greatest of these is Charity.

Praise GOD, after reading this Chapter, you can see that love sets an example, love has a walk – behavior, love has a law it abides by, and it has Courage. Love has Characteristic upon Characteristic if you really think about it. GOD gave me those first four Characteristics, but I needed more. So I asked GOD for more Characteristics to write about and this is what GOD gave me. HE said love is:

-L-ovingkindness -

-O-vercoming -

-V-ictoriously -

-E- ternally -

So I said thank you Jesus, I can write my next four Chapters on those Characteristics of Love.

Loving-kindness overcoming victoriously eternally. Praise GOD, that is powerful, and it is right in line with verse 8 of the passage I just gave you. First CORINTHIANS 13:8, it says; Charity (Love) "never" faileth.

Glory to GOD!

I can tell you one thing dear Christians, if GOD ever speaks to you and tells you something, you will be able to go to the Word of GOD and back it up one hundred percent. If you cannot support it with the Word of GOD, you may need to disregard it, because it may be your own self or an unclean Spirit. But, that is something you can bank on, if GOD says it, you will be able to support it with HIS Holy Word.

I told you that the Lord showed me three power action words in First CORINTHIANS 13:13, faith, hope, love....These are action words for every believer to apply to our lives. Once we do, we will begin to grow Spiritually into the people of GOD that HE has called us to be.

Praise GOD, love is the greatest of all. You can have monster faith and no love, and be the weakest Christian in the world. You can have hope on top of hope and no love, and you won't ever accomplish anything. Love is the greatest of all. When you have got love in your life, then you will be victorious in all you do for GOD. You see, you may have an awesome anointing on you for the gift of healing, and someone may come to you to lay hands on them and pray for their healing. You may do it, and say a beautiful mouthful of prayer. But, if you really don't love that person enough to really want to see them healed, that prayer may fall to the floor as soon as you pray it.

That is what this passage is saying in First CORINTHIANS 13:8, it says:

v. 8, Charity never faileth: but whether there be Prophecies, they shall fail; whether there be tongues, they shall cease; whether there be knowledge, it shall vanish away.

This verse is not saying that these gifts won't be in practice forever, what it is saying is, without love, GOD'S (Agape), fruit of the Spirit kind of love, these gifts won't function victoriously. The first phrase in this verse says, "Love never fails". So the point is, these gifts will never fail as long as love is the power source.

A lot of people use this passage to say that those gifts are not available for the Church today, that is way out in left field. That would be like saying GOD is not available for the Church today. Dear Christian people, HEBREWS 13:8 says:

v. 8, Jesus Christ is the same yesterday, today, and forever.

Don't you follow any doctrine that says those gifts ceased to exist. The Bible says in first CORINTHIANS 12:31:

v. 31, But covet earnestly the best gifts: and yet shew I unto you a more excellent way.

It says to Covet the best gifts, and then it goes into Chapter thirteen on love to show you that you must be functioning in the fruit of the Spirit kind of love for any of those gifts to prosper. But it does not imply that GOD has taken them away from the Church by any means. Let me tell you dear Christian people, the reason GOD was able to use Moses so greatly for the Children of Israel, was because Moses really loved them. That is why GOD was able to work all of those miracles through Moses. Moses loved the people so much, that he would kill for them and he loved them enough to go to hell for them. Let me prove my point to you.

Let's look at this passage where Moses loved the people so much that he killed a man for them. EXODUS 2:11-12, it says:

v. 11, And it came to pass in those days, when Moses was grown, that he went out unto his brethren, and looked on their burdens: and he spied an Egyptian smiting an Hebrew, one of his brethren.

v. 12, And he looked this way and that way, and when he saw that there was no man, he slew the Egyptian, and hid him in the sand.

Dear people, "that" is how much Moses loved his people. That is why GOD was able to use Moses so mightily.

Glory to GOD!

Let's look at another passage where Moses proved to love his people, even to the point of going to hell for them. Look at EXODUS 32:1-32, it says:

v. 1, And when the people saw that Moses delayed to come down out of the mount, the people gathered themselves together unto Aaron, and said unto him, up, make us Gods, which shall go before us; for as for this Moses, the man that brought us up out of the land of Egypt, we wot not what is become of him.

v. 2, And Aaron said unto them, Break off the golden earrings, which are in the ears of your wives, of your sons, and of your daughters, and bring them unto me.

v. 3, And all the people brake off the golden earrings which were in their ears, and brought them unto Aaron.

v. 4, And he received them at their hand, and fashioned it with a graving tool, after he had made it a molten calf: and they said, these be thy gods, O Israel, which brought thee up out of the land of Egypt.

v. 5, And when Aaron saw it he built an alter before it; and Aaron made proclamation, and said. To morrow is a feast to the Lord.

v. 6, And they rose up early on the morrow, and offered burnt offerings, and brought peace offerings; and the people sat down to eat and to drink, and rose up to play.

v. 7, And the Lord said unto Moses, Go, get thee down, for thy people, which thou broughtest out of the land of Egypt, have corrupted themselves:

v. 8, They have turned aside quickly out of the way which I commanded them: they have made them a molten calf, and have worshipped it, and have sacrificed thereunto, and said, these be thy gods, O Israel, which have brought thee up out of the land of Egypt.

v. 9, And the Lord said unto Moses, I have seen this people, and behold, it is a stiffnecked people:

v. 10, Now therefore let me alone, that my wrath may wax hot against them, and that I may consume them: and I will make of thee a great nation.

v. 11, And Moses besought the Lord his God, and said, Lord, why doth thy wrath wax hot against thy people, which thou hast brought forth out of the land of Egypt with great power, and with a mighty hand?

v. 12, Wherefore should the Egyptians speak, and say, For mischief did he bring them out, to slay them in the mountains, and to consume them from the face of the earth? Turn from thy fierce wrath, and repent of this evil against thy people.

v. 13, Remember Abraham, Isaac, and Israel, thy servants, to whom thou swarest by thy own self, and saidst unto them, I will multiply your seed as the stars of heaven, and all this land that I have spoken of will I give unto your seed, and they shall inherit it for ever.

v. 14, And the Lord repented of the evil which he thought to do unto his people.

v. 15, And Moses turned, and went down from the mount, and the two tables of the testimony were in his hand: the tables were written on both their sides; on the one side and on the other were they written.

v. 16, And the tables were the work of God, and the writing was the writing of God, graven upon the tables.

v. 17, And when Joshua heard the noise of the people as they shouted, he said unto Moses, There is a noise of war in the camp.

v. 18, And he said, It is not the voice of them, that shout for mastery, neither is it the voice of them that cry for being overcome: but the noise of them that sing do I hear.

v. 19, And it came to pass, as soon as he came nigh unto the camp, that he saw the calf, and the dancing: and Moses' anger waxed hot, and he cast the tables out of his hands, and brake them beneath the mount.

v. 20, And he took the calf which they had made, and burnt it in the fire, and ground it to powder, and strawed it upon the water, and made the Children of Israel drink of it.

v. 21, And Moses said unto Aaron, what did this people unto thee, that thou hast brought so great a sin upon them?

v. 22, And Aaron said, let not the anger of my lord wax hot: thou knowest the people, that they are set on mischief.

v. 23, For they said unto me, make us gods, which shall go before us: for as for this Moses, the man that brought us up out of the land of Egypt, we wot not what is become of him.

v. 24, And I said unto them, whosoever hath any gold, let them break it off. So they gave it me: then I cast it into the fire, and there came out this calf.

v. 25, And when Moses saw that the people were naked,; (for Aaron had made them naked unto their shame among their enemies:)

v. 26, Then Moses stood in the gate of the camp, and said, who is on the Lord's side? let him come unto me. And all the sons of Levi gathered themselves together unto him.

v. 27, And he said unto them, Thus saith the Lord God of Israel, put every man his sword by his side, and go in and out from gate to gate throughout the camp, and slay every man his brother, and every man his companion, and every man his neighbor.

v. 28, And the Children of Levi did according to the word of Moses: and there fell of the people that day about three thousand men.

v. 29, For Moses had said, consecrate yourselves to day to the Lord, even every man upon his son, and upon his brother; that he may bestow upon you a blessing this day.

v. 30, And it came to pass on the morrow, that Moses said unto the people, ye have sinned a great sin: and now I will go up unto the Lord; Peradventure I shall make an atonement for your sin.

v. 31, And Moses returned unto the Lord, and said, oh this people have sinned a great sin, and have made them gods of gold.

v. 32, yet now, if thou wilt forgive their sin; and if not, blot me, I pray thee, out of thy book which thou hast written.

Glory to GOD Christians! That is love!

Moses knew that GOD had written his name in the Lamb's book of life. Moses knew that GOD had something in store for him even after he died. But he loved those people so much, that he asked GOD to forgive them and blot him out of the book that he had written. Moses was willing to kill for them and go to hell for the people. GOD had even offered to make Moses a great nation. GOD said in verse 10,

v. 10, Now therefore let me alone, that my wrath may wax hot against them, and that I may consume them: and I will make of thee a great nation.

Praise GOD! GOD said to Moses, let me alone, let me destroy them, let me consume them and I will make of you (Moses) a great nation. But, Moses loved the people so much that he stood in the gap and asked GOD to have mercy on them for what they had done.

Precious People of GOD, I have just showed you the GOD inspired kind of love that GOD wants to instill into all of us Christians. Moses loved the people so much, that he was willing to kill for them and that he was willing to die and go to hell for them. Praise GOD Almighty, that is a Divine Revelation Of Love.

Chapter Six

The Loving-Kindness of Love

I SAIAH 63:7

I will mention the lovingkindness of the Lord, and the Praises of the Lord, according to all that the Lord hath bestowed on us, and the great goodness toward the house of Israel, which he hath bestowed on them according to his mercies, and according to the multitude of his lovingkindness.

Fellow Christians, as we examine the next Characteristic of Love, allow me to note that some people believe that GOD is the only one with this Characteristic. It is the Loving-Kindness of love, which is the next Characteristic that we will study. Let me tell you upfront that loving-kindness is indeed obtainable in the Christian life. It is not just a thing that only GOD can do, and you cannot. Now, I will say that we must always keep in mind that it is always GOD working through us.

We are never, ever to claim that we did this or that, we are never, ever to say I healed a person or I worked a miracle or I cast out a demon or anything that the Bible teaches us is GOD'S doing.

Let's look at what Jesus said in the book of JOHN Chapter 15:1-5, it says:

v. 1, I am the true vine, and my Father is the husbandman.

v. 2, Every branch in me that beareth not fruit he taketh away: and every branch that beareth fruit, he purgeth it, that it may bring forth more fruit.

v. 3, Now ye are clean through the word which I have spoken unto you.

v. 4, Abide in me, and I in you. As the branch cannot bear fruit of itself, except it abide in the vine; no more can ye, except ye abide in me.

v. 5, I am the vine, ye are the branches: He that abideth in me, and I in him, the same bringeth forth much fruit: for without me ye can do nothing.

Well Christian People, that is pretty clear right there isn't it? Jesus made it pretty clear, HE said I am the vine in verse one, then HE says in verse four, As the branch (cannot) bear fruit of "itself", no more can ye except ye abide in me. Then look at what HE (Jesus) goes on to say at the end of verse five, HE said, "for without me ye can do nothing". So you see, my point is very clear, none of what we do in the Supernatural is of our own power. We can do nothing without Him, "Jesus".

But Praise GOD dear people, because the flip side of this is, we can do all things in HIM! Let'slook at a very popular verse to prove my point, PHILIPPIANS 4:13, it says:

v. 13, I can do all things through Christ which strengtheneth me.

Glory to GOD! We can do all things....That is through Christ which strengthens us. Hallelujah!

You can do all things....That is through Christ which strengthens you. Always remember that dear people, it is always HIM and none of us. Please let me give you an example of what could happen when we start trying to do things in our strength. Look at ACTS Chapter nineteen, 19:13-16, it says:

v. 13, Then certain of the vegabond Jews, exorcists, took upon them to call over them which had evil spirits the name of the Lord Jesus, saying, we adjure you by Jesus whom Paul preacheth.

v. 14, And there were seven sons of one Sceva, a Jew, and Chief of the Priests, which did so.

v. 15, And the evil spirit answered and said, Jesus I know, and Paul I know; but who are ye?

v. 16, And the man in whom the evil spirit was leaped on them, and overcame them, and prevailed against them, so that they fled out of that house naked and wounded.

My point is, we have to know where the Supernatural Power comes from. Look at verse 13, they said we adjure you (evil spirit) by Jesus whom Paul preaches. They thought they themselves could cast out the evil spirit with the power of someone that somebody else had. Those people could not cast that evil spirit out because they themselves did not have Jesus in their lives. Some of them were even Spiritual leaders, it says in verse 14, that the Chief Priests were there also.

My Dear Christian Friend, always keep in mind that it is never our own doings. No where in the Bible does it say that we can do Supernatural things ourselves. Jesus said without HIM we could do absolutely nothing. But Praise GOD fellow Christians because (with

HIM) we can do all things. We can lay our hands on the sick and they will recover, we can speak with tongues, we can do miracles. Let me give you some examples of what we can do in Christ, not ourselves, but in Christ. Look at MARK 16:15-20, it says:

v. 15, And he said unto them, Go ye into all the world, and preach the gospel to every creature.

v. 16, He that believeth and is baptized shall be saved, but he that believeth not shall be damned.

v. 17, And these signs shall follow them that believe, In my name shall they cast out devils, they shall speak with new tongues;

v. 18, They shall take up serpents, and if they drink any deadly thing, it shall not hurt them; they shall lay hands on the sick, and they shall recover.

v. 19, So then after the Lord had spoken unto them, he was received up into heaven, and sat on the right hand of God.

v. 20, And they went forth, and preached everywhere, the Lord working with them, and confirming the word with signs following. Amen.

This is an awesome example of a lot of the great supernatural things GOD will do through us. But, notice in verse 17, it says, In my name they will do these things. So you see, we do not have the supernatural power to do anything. The power source is in the name of Jesus. Then it tells you in verse 20, that the Lord was working with them and doing the signs. The Lord is the one who does the miracles, through us.

Thus, what our study has shown us is this, even though some people believe that this Characteristic of Love, (The Loving-Kindness of love) is something that only GOD can practice. The Bible shows that in the name of Jesus, we can indeed show loving-kindness. It will always be the Spirit of GOD working through us and not we ourselves, but we can experience the loving-kindness of GOD. We are capable of showing loving-kindness in our every day lives with the help of the Holy Spirit.

In our opening verse, you can see some of what loving-kindness is. Let's look at it again, ISAIAH 63:7, it says:

v. 7, I will mention the lovingkindness of the Lord, and the praises of the Lord, according to all that the Lord hath bestowed on us, and the great goodness toward the house of Israel, which he hath bestowed on them according to his mercies, and according to the multitude of his lovingkindness.

As you look at this verse, it speaks of the Lord's loving-kindness. It says, "I will mention thy lovingkindness", and it says "according to the multitude of his lovingkindness". This proves just exactly what I have been showing you. It is "HIS" loving-kindness that "HE" shows through us. Actually, loving- kindness is mercy, GOD tells us and helps us to have mercy on one another. Actually, mercy is a gift of the Spirit. GOD tells us to lay hands on the sick for healing, that is loving-kindness, GOD tells us to love one another, that is loving-kindness, GOD tells us to practice the fruit of the Spirit in GALATIANS Chapter five, it says, to have love, joy, peace, long-suffering, gentleness, goodness, faith, meekness, temperance. All of these are action words of loving-kindness that GOD will work through us.

Praise GOD People!

Every time you tell someone Jesus loves them, you are practicing the loving-kindness of GOD. Every time you lay hands on the sick for healing, you are practicing the loving-kindness of GOD. Every time you give someone a love offering, you are practicing the loving-kindness of GOD. Every time you have mercy on someone who has really done you wrong, you are practicing the loving-kindness of GOD.

That goes back to following the examples of GOD. Jesus gives us examples on top of examples in the Gospels, MATTHEW, MARK, LUKE AND JOHN. Not to mention GOD gives us the same examples all throughout the Bible. We are to follow GOD'S examples of how to love. We are to follow GOD'S examples of how to have mercy. We are to follow GOD'S examples of how to teach. We are to follow GOD'S examples of how to practice goodness. And Praise GOD, we are to follow GOD'S examples of showing loving-kindness in our everyday lives.

Let's look at another verse that shows that we are to follow HIS examples. Look at 1st Peter, 2:21, it says:

v. 21, For even hereunto were ye called: because Christ also suffered for us, leaving us an example, that ye should follow his steps.

Glory to GOD Dear People!

The entire life of Jesus Christ is a divine example of how to practice GOD'S loving-kindness in our lives. This verse says Jesus set us an example in HIS suffering, (That ye should follow his steps). You see, Jesus suffered for us. "That" is loving-kindness in action my dear fellow Christian. And this very verse that we just looked at, tells us very clearly that this is an example that HE left us, that we should follow HIS steps. That is HIS example!

We should love the way Jesus loved. We should talk the way Jesus talked. We should walk the way Jesus walked. We should set examples the way Jesus set them for us. Everything we see GOD do concerning loving-kindness, from GENESIS to REVELATION, we are to follow those divine examples of HIS loving-kindness, and with HIS help, we can do all things the way GOD does them, through Christ which strengthens us.

Glory to GOD! Another powerful Characteristic of Love is, The Loving-Kindness of Love....

Chapter Seven

The Overcomingness of Love

1 st JOHN 5:4

For whatsoever is born of God overcometh the world: and this is the victory that overcometh the world, even our faith.

Dear People of GOD, the next Characteristic of Love that we will look at is the overcomingness of love. It is a characteristic that you will always experience if you are really and truly practicing the fruit of the Spirit GOD-like kind of love that the Bible teaches us to have.

Let me tell you something People of GOD, our GOD is the ultimate overcomer. So if we are rooted and grounded in GOD'S love, then we will be walking in this here Characteristic of Love. Then we will learn how to apply GOD'S Holy Word, (The Bible) to any situation that we may face, and we will overcome it, as long as we apply

GOD'S Word. The Bible even goes as far as saying GOD is love. Let's look at it in 1st JOHN 4:16, it says:

v. 16, And we have known and believe the love that God hath to us. God is love; and he that dwelleth in love dwelleth in God, and God in him.

Glory to GOD! GOD is love! Dear people, according to this verse, GOD Himself is love. Now you know, GOD is the only ultimate overcomer. So then if GOD is love, and one of the Characteristics of GOD is HIS overcomingness, then it is very GOD inspired and Biblical to say that a very important Characteristic of Love is the overcomingness of love. Let's look back at our opening verse again. 1st JOHN 5:4, it says:

v. 4, For whatsoever is born of God overcometh the world: and this is the victory that overcometh the world, even our faith.

Precious people, you are the whatsoever in this verse. What it is saying is this, whatever this world may bring your way, you can overcome it if you are born of GOD. So if you are born of GOD, then my dear friend, you are born of love. So if you are born of GOD and you can walk in the overcomingness of GOD, then if you are born of love then you can walk in the overcomingness of love and overcome any bad situation that this old world may bring across your path. Hallelujah!

Let me give you another example that shows very clearly that if you are not fully loving the way GOD wants you to, you will not be an overcomer in that situation. Look at it in 1st CORINTHIANS 13:1-3, it says: (Remember Charity is love)

v. 1, Though I speak with the tongues of men and of angels, and have not Charity (love) I am become as sounding brass, or a tinkling cymbal.

v. 2, And though I have the gift of Prophecy, and understand all mysteries, and all knowledge; and though I have all faith, so that I could remove mountains, and have not Charity, (love) I am nothing.

v. 3, And though I bestow all my goods to feed the poor, and though I give my body to be burned, and have not Charity, (love) it profiteth me nothing.

What this passage is saying dear people is, if you don't apply love to every situation you face, then you won't be an overcomer in that issue. Look, it says though I speak with the tongues of men and angels and "have not love", it is nothing. In other words, if you do not truly love the person you are speaking to, then whatever knowledge you share with them, or whatever encouragement you give them, won't be worth two cents. It won't prosper, it won't help them at all, because the Power of GOD won't be behind it.

Look again, it says, though I have the gift of Prophecy. If you really don't love that person you give a word of Prophecy to, it will not overcome for them. It won't prosper. It says though I have faith that could remove mountains. If I don't have love, that faith won't overcome that mountain. It says faith that "could" remove mountains, that means that without love, it "could not" remove mountains. It goes on to say in verse three, and though I give all my goods to the poor. If I really don't love that poor person, it is nothing. It even goes as far as to say even if I give my body to be burned (killed for someone), if I really don't love them, it is nothing.

Dear Christian, what this is saying is, that one of the most important Characteristics of Love is the overcomingness. It is saying if you really have the fruit of the Spirit kind of love, and you apply it to any situation that this life brings your way, then you will overcome that situation. Love is the overcoming agent of "all" of our problems. Praise GOD dear people.

Let's look at some more Scripture to show that love is an overcomer. Look at REVELATION 12:11, it says:

v. 11, And they overcame him by the blood of the Lamb, and by the word of their testimony; and they loved not their lives unto the death.

This is a powerful verse to show the overcomingness of love. It says that they, (the Christians) overcame the devil by the blood of the Lamb. You see, the blood itself is the ultimate expression of love. The reason so, is because it expresses the love of the Lamb. Praise GOD! That is why you will see many Christians praying about things and pleading the blood over that situation, to help them overcome it. That is why you will see many Christians praying and pleading the blood of Jesus over somebody for protection from the devil. That is why you will see people pleading the blood of Jesus over lost loved ones for Salvation. That is why you will see people praying and pleading the blood of Jesus over their homes and financial investments and everything they may face in this life. The blood of the Lamb is indeed the ultimate expression of the love of the Lamb, and it has the full explosive power of overcomingness to overcome any situation this life may bring your way.

Glory to GOD!

Let's look at another powerful passage of the overcomingness of love, overcoming a serious situation. Look at 1st SAMUEL 17:45-51, it says:

v. 45, Then said David to the Philistine, Thou comest to me with a sword, and with a spear, and with a shield: but I come to thee in the name of the Lord of hosts, the God of the armies of Israel, whom thou hast defied.

v. 46, This day will the Lord deliver thee into mine hand; and I will smite thee, and take thine head from thee; and I will give the carcases of the host of the Philistines this day unto the fowls of the air, and to the wild beasts of the earth; that all the earth may know that there is a God in Israel.

v. 47, And all this assembly shall know that the Lord saveth not with sword and spear: for the battle is the Lord's and he will give you into our hands.

v. 48, And it came to pass, when the Philistines arose, and came and drew nigh to meet David, that David hasted, and ran toward the army to meet the Philistine.

v. 49, And David put his hand in his bag, and took thence a stone, and slang it, and smote the Philistine in his forehead; that the stone sunk into his forehead and he fell upon his face to the earth.

v. 50, So David prevailed over the Philistine with a sling and with a stone, and smote the Philistine, and slew him; but there was no sword in the hand of David.

v. 51, Therefore David ran, and stood upon the Philistine, and took his sword, and drew it out of the sheath thereof, and slew him, and cut off his head therewith. And when the Philistines saw their champion was dead, they fled.

You see, David had already been anointed King before this ever took place. And GOD knew that David loved HIS people, that is why HE chose him for their King. David had the people of Israel on his mind when he faced the giant. Look at verse 45, at what David said to the giant, he said; I come to thee in the name of the Lord of hosts, the God of the armies of Israel, whom thou hast defied. You see, the giant didn't challenge GOD, he challenged the people. David had the people on his heart. David loved the people and he told the giant, I come to you in the name of the people that I love's GOD. That is basically what David was saying. He was saying, you have defied (challenged) the people I love, and I come to you in the name of our GOD. To defy, means to challenge, the giant challenged the people David and GOD loved. Praise GOD! David loved those people, and he "overcame" the giant with the "overcoming" power of love.

People of GOD, let me give you one more excellent passage to show the overcoming power of love. Look at the Gospel of JOHN, 16:33, it says:

v. 33, These things I have spoken unto you, that in me ye might have peace. In the world ye shall have tribulation: but be of good cheer: I have overcome the world.

This is a powerful passage of the overcomingness of love. Jesus is love, because HE is GOD, and GOD is love. Look at what Jesus tells us in this verse. HE said "in me" ye might have peace. It is in HIM that we will overcome anything that comes against our peace. Jesus said in this passage, that in this world we would have tribulation; but in HIM we would have peace. Then HE tells us to be of good cheer, because HE has overcome the world. So actually what Jesus is saying is, that HE loves us so much that HE Himself has took on and overcame any situation that you and I could ever face in this world. Jesus is saying that HE loves us so much, that we will overcome anything, because we are in HIM, and HE has already overcome it for us. "That" dear people is why we can fully trust in the unfailing overcomingness of love, because Jesus is the ultimate example of love and HE promised us in HIM we will overcome. So you see dear people, that another powerful Characteristic of Love is The Overcomingness of Love.

Glory to GOD!

Chapter Eight

The Victoriousness of Love

1 st JOHN 5:4

For whatsoever is born of God overcometh the world: and this is the victory that overcometh the world, even our faith.

People of GOD, I ask you to pay close attention to this chapter. Because the last chapter we covered was on the overcomingness of love. This chapter we will cover a similar Characteristic and that is The Victoriousness of Love. You may say well what on earth is the difference in the words overcome and victory. That is the same thing I said until the Lord showed me.

So let me show you what the Lord showed me. Look at JOB Chapter One, it says:

v. 1, There was a man in the land of Uz, whose name was Job; and that man was perfect and upright, and one that feared God, and eschewed evil.

v. 2, And there were born unto him seven sons and three daughters.

v. 3, His substance also was seven thousand sheep, and three thousand camels, and five hundred yoke of oxen, and five hundred she asses, and a very great household; so that this man was the greatest of all the men of the east.

v. 4, And his sons went and feasted in their houses, every one his day; and sent and called for their three sisters to eat and drink with them.

v. 5, And it was so, when the days of their feasting were gone about, that Job sent and sanctified them, and rose up early in the morning, and offered burnt offerings according to the number of them all: for Job said, It may be that my sons have sinned, and cursed God in their hearts. Thus did Job continually.

v. 6, Now there was a day when the sons of God came to present themselves before the Lord, and Satan came also among them.

v. 7, And the Lord said unto Satan, whence comest thou? Then Satan answered the Lord and said, From going to and fro in the earth, and from walking up and down in it.

v. 8, And the Lord said unto Satan, Hast thou considered my servant Job, that there is none like him in the earth, a perfect and an upright man, one that feareth God, and escheweth evil?

v. 9, Then Satan answered the Lord, and said, Doth Job fear God for nought?

v. 10, Hast not thou made an hedge about him, and about his house, and about all that he hath on every side? Thou hast blessed the work of his hands, and his substance is increased in the land.

v. 11, But put forth thine hand now, and touch all that he hath, and he will curse thee to thy face.

v. 12, And the Lord said unto Satan, Behold, all that he hath is in thy power; only upon himself put not forth thine hand. So Satan went forth from the presence of the Lord.

v. 13, And there was a day when his sons and his daughters were eating and drinking wine in their eldest brother's house:

v. 14, And there came a messenger unto Job, and said, The oxen were plowing, and the asses feeding beside them:

v. 15, And the Sabeans fell upon them, and took them away; yea, they have slain the servants with the edge of the sword; and I only am escaped alone to tell thee.

v. 16, While he was yet speaking, there came also another, and said, The Chaldeans made out three bands, and fell upon the camels, and have carried them away, yea, and slain the servants with the edge of the sword; and I only am escaped alone to tell thee.

v. 18, While he was yet speaking, there came also another, and said, Thy sons and thy daughters were eating and drinking wine in their eldest brother's house:

v. 19, And, behold, there came a great wind from the wilderness, and smote the four corners of the house, and it fell upon the young men, and they are dead; and I only am escaped alone to tell thee,

v. 20, The Job arose, and rent his mantle, and shaved his head, and fell down upon the ground, and worshipped,

v. 21, And said, naked came I out of my Mother's womb, and naked shall I return thither: the Lord gave, and the Lord hath taken away; blessed be the name of the Lord.

v. 22, In all this Job sinned not, nor charged God foolishly.

Dear Christian People, this is where Job overcame this situation. In verse 22, he said the Lord gave, the Lord hath taken away, blessed be the name of the Lord. What Job was saying was, I'm putting it in GOD'S hands, I'm still going to worship and bless GOD no matter what. That is how Job overcame it all, but he still didn't have the victory. Satan came at Job again in Chapter 2, and made him very sick. But Job overcame that also. Look at what happened, JOB 2:9-10, it says:

v. 9, Then said his wife unto him, Dost thou still retain thine integrity? Curse God, and die.

v. 10, But he said unto her, Thou speakest as one of the foolish women speaketh. What? Shall we receive good at the hand of God, and shall we not receive evil? In all this did not Job sin with his lips.

Glory to GOD People!

What Job was saying here is, that GOD is in control, I am going to trust HIM in the good times and in the bad times. You see, by remaining faithful, Job overcame all of that, he put it in GOD'S hands and continued to trust GOD. But he still did not have the victory. You see, you canovercome a situation but you won't actually have the victory until what you lost is restored.

If you would like, you can read all of JOB. But I'll tell you that everything that happens from Chapter 2 to Chapter 42 evolves around Job's grief. My dear friend, we are humans, GOD created us with emotions, and when we experience things like Job did, we are going to grieve about it. That is human nature. So although Job overcame it, he still grieved about it. Look at what it says in Chapter 2:13, it says:

v. 13, So they sat down with him upon the ground seven days and seven nights, and none spake a word unto him: for they saw that his grief was very great.

People of GOD, it says that they saw that his grief was very great. Then look at what Job himself said in Chapter 6:1-2, it says:

v. 1, But Job answered and said,

v. 2, Oh that my grief were thoroughly weighed, and my calamity laid in the balances together.

Precious People of GOD, It is GOD given human nature to grieve when we face things like Job faced. If someone says they do not grieve, then something is very wrong with their emotion thermometer. My point is, that there is a difference in overcoming and having the victory over a situation. Job overcame his situation by putting it in GOD'S hands. GOD allowed Job to grieve concerning the situation. Then in the final chapter of Job, after Job had finished grieving, GOD gave him the victory. Let's look at it in JOB 42:10-13, it says:

v. 10, And the Lord turned the captivity of Job, when he prayed for his friends: also the Lord gave Job twice as much as he had before.

v. 11, Then came there unto him all his brethren, and all his sisters, and all they that had been of his acquaintance before, and did eat bread with him in his house: and they bemoaned him, and comforted him over all the evil that the Lord had brought upon him: every man also gave him a piece of money, and every one an earring of gold.

v. 12, So the Lord blessed the latter end of Job more than his beginning: for he had fourteen thousand sheep, and six thousand camels, and a thousand yoke of oxen, and a thousand asses.

v. 13, He had also seven sons and three daughters.

Praise GOD! Dear people, you see there is an obvious difference in the overcomingness and the victoriousness of love. As you have seen in the life of Job, you really don't have the victory until all is restored. Job really didn't get his same children back, but he really didn't lose them either. You must keep in mind that although they were killed in the storm, that does not mean that they ceased to exist. Actually, GOD just took them on to Heaven and Job would see them again when he passed on over into Heaven. So actually he never really lost them. But he had to grieve their absence.

GOD restored Job with ten more children, and twice as much material property as he had to start with. Praise GOD! That is the victory. You see, we as Christians have the victory in Jesus. Jesus took back everything that Satan had taken from GOD'S people when HE died on the Cross. The only thing Satan has now, is what the non Christians have allowed him to take from them. Let me give you an example of how Jesus won the victory over Satan for us. Look at what the Bible says about Satan in 1st PETER 5:8, it says:

v. 8, Be sober, be vigilant; because your adversary the devil, as a roaring lion, walketh about, seeking whom he may devour.

Have you ever seen a cartoon where the little character steps on a board or something, and it flies up and hits him in the face? Then he turns and smiles and his teeth just start falling out, "tink, tink, tink," then all of them just fall out. Well that is what happened to Satan, as Jesus was up on the Cross for you and I. Satan was smiling and laughing his head off. But Glory to GOD, as each drop of blood hit the ground, old Satan's smile began to fade and his teeth began to fall out. Then that monstrous roar became a passive meow as each one of his teeth hit the ground, "tink, tink, tink". As each drop of blood hit the ground, another tooth fell out.

You see, Jesus took everything back from him for us Christians. Once we give our lives to GOD, and allow Jesus to come into our hearts, HE then starts restoring all that the devil took from us, and giving us the victory over the devil.

Precious People, Moses loved the People of GOD to the point of going to hell for them. But GOD loves us more than that, GOD would not go to hell for us, but HE sure went through it to keep us from going there. GOD loves us so much, that HE couldn't stand to see us defeated and beat down by the devil any longer. So HE, Himself, in HIS love, got the victory for us and as we come to HIM, HE will restore all to us and twice as much as the devil took from us.

Praise GOD! That is The Victoriousness of Love.

Chapter Nine

The Eternality of Love

H EBREWS 9:14

How much more shall the blood of Christ, who through the eternal Spirit offered himself with out spot to God, Purge your conscience from dead works to serve the living God?

People of GOD, the next Characteristic of Love I want to examine is: The Eternality of Love.

Love is an eternal force that will never ever fail. In our opening verse, the writer of HEBREWS mentions the eternal Spirit. Let's look at it again in HEBREWS 9:14-15, it says:

v. 14, How much more shall the blood of Christ, who through the eternal Spirit offered himself without spot to God, Purge your conscience from dead works to serve the living God.

v. 15, And for this cause he is the mediator of the new testament, that by means of death, for the redemption of the transgressions that were under the first testament, they which are called might receive the promise of eternal inheritance.

So you see dear Christian people, that verse 14 speaks of the eternal Spirit of GOD, and verse 15 speaks of the eternal inheritance of GOD. We know that love is the fruit of the Spirit. It is fruit of the eternal Spirit. Love is part of the eternal inheritance mentioned in verse 15. Love is Eternal because GOD is Eternal and love is a characteristic of GOD. So by this we see our next Characteristic, The Eternality of Love.

People of GOD, the Bible says in one place, that GOD Himself is love. Let's look at it again in 1st JOHN 4:16, it says:

v. 16, And we have known and believed the love that God hath to us. God is love; and he that dwelleth in love dwelleth in God, and God in him.

So you can see by this verse, that the Bible goes as far as to say, GOD is love. And we know GOD

is Eternal, so we can also know that love is Eternal. Let's look at another verse to prove my point, where the Bible refers to GOD as love. Look at 1st

JOHN 4:7-8, it says:

v. 7, Beloved let us love one another: for love is of God; and every one that loveth is born of God, and knoweth God.

v. 8, He that loveth not knoweth not God, for God is love.

Fellow Christians that is pretty clear, it says very clearly, Love is of GOD and GOD is love, right here in these two verses. I would also like to point out something in this passage to assure you that you can be reborn or born again, here and now in this life. Some people teach that the new birth does not take place until we die and go to Heaven. Don't you ever believe any doctrine like that. Look at verse Seven again, 1st JOHN 4:7, it says:

v. 7, Beloved, let us love one another: for love is of God; and every one that loveth is born of God, and knoweth God.

Praise GOD Christian people, that verse right there shows very clearly that everyone that loves, is born, that means reborn, or born again, of GOD and knows GOD. Don't you let anybody tell you that you cannot be born again until you die. That is a lie from that old toothless devil, and you better not believe it.

The rebirth takes place when you accept Jesus into your life as your Lord and Savior. Right then you begin to enjoy your Eternal inheritance. You begin to enjoy your Eternal life of love as soon as you accept Jesus into your life as your Lord and Savior, and don't you let anyone tell you differently.

Please allow me to show you some Scriptures that prove that Jesus is the Eternal Son of GOD. Look at the Gospel of JOHN 1:1-3, it says:

v. 1, In the beginning was the word, and the word was with God, and the word was God.

v. 2, The same was in the beginning with God.

v. 3, All things were made by him; and without him was not any thing made that was made.

Praise GOD! Jesus is the word. Some people will argue till they are blue in the face that Jesus is not the word. Don't you go for that one either. Look at verse three again very closely, it says:

v. 3, All things were made by him; and without him was not any thing made that was made.

It says all things were made by "him" without "him" nothing was made that was made. It is pretty obvious that this passage is referring to the word as a "him". And Praise GOD, Jesus is that "him" the living word, the walking and talking word that became flesh and dwelt among us. Praise GOD! The Eternal Son of GOD, the Eternal Son of love, Jesus is the Eternality of love also.

Glory to GOD!

Let's look at another verse that proves that Jesus has been around since Creation and will indeed be around Eternally. Let's look at COLOSSIANS 1:14-17, it says:

v. 14, In whom we have redemption through his blood, even the forgiveness of sins:

v. 15, who is the image of the invisible God, the firstborn of every creature:

v. 16, For by him were all things created, that are in heaven, and that are in earth, visible and invisible, whether they be thrones, or dominions, or principalities, or powers: all things were created by him, and for him:

v. 17, And he is before all things, and by him all things consist.

Dear People of GOD, this passage shows very clearly that Jesus has been around since the beginning. It says in verse 14:

v. 14, In whom we have redemption through his blood, even the forgiveness of sins:

So you see, it has to be talking about Jesus because it says we have redemption through HIS blood. There is no other blood for mankind to have redemption through except the Precious blood of Jesus. The Eternal Son of love. Glory to GOD!

Dear People of GOD, let's look at one more Chapter that proves very clearly to us that everything concerning the Eternality of Love and of Jesus that we have discussed so far, is true. Look at the Book of EPHESIANS Chapter One, it says:

v. 1, Paul an apostle of Jesus Christ by the will of God, to the saints which are at Ephesus, and to the faithful in Christ Jesus:

v. 2, Grace be to you, and peace, from God our Father, and from the Lord Jesus Christ.

v. 3, Blessed be the God and Father of our Lord Jesus Christ, who hath blessed us with all Spiritual blessings in heavenly places in Christ:

v. 4, According as he hath chosen us in him before the foundation of the world, that we should be holy and without blame before him in love.

v. 5, Having Predestinated us unto the adoption of Children by Jesus Christ to himself, according to the good pleasure of his will.

v. 6, To the Praise of the glory of his grace, wherein he hath made us accepted in the beloved.

v. 7, In whom we have redemption through his blood, the forgiveness of sins, according to the riches of his grace;

v. 8, wherein he hath abounded toward us in all wisdom and prudence;

v. 9, Having made known unto us the mystery of his will, according to his good pleasure which he hath purposed in himself:

v. 10, That in the dispensation of the fulness of times he might gather together in one all things in Christ, both which are in heaven, and which are on earth; even in him:

v. 11, In whom also we have obtained an inheritance, being Predestinated according to the purpose of him who worketh all things after the counsel of his own will:

v. 12, That we should be to the Praise of his glory, who first trusted in Christ.

v. 13, In whom ye also trusted, after that ye heard the word of truth, the gospel of your Salvation: in whom also after that ye believed, ye were sealed with that Holy Spirit of Promise,

v. 14, which is the earnest of our inheritance until the redemption of the purchased possession, unto the Praise of his glory.

v. 15, Wherefore I also, after I heard of your faith in the Lord Jesus, and love unto all the Saints,

v. 16, Cease not to give thanks for you, making mention of you in my prayers;

v. 17, That the God of our Lord Jesus Christ, the Father of glory, may give unto you the Spirit of wisdom and revelation in the knowledge of him:

v. 18, The eyes of your understanding being enlightened; that ye may know what is the hope of his calling, and what the riches of the glory of his inheritance in the Saints,

v. 19, And what is the exceeding greatness of his power to usward who believe, according to the working of his mighty power;

v. 20, which he wrought in Christ, when he raised him from the dead, and set him at his own right hand in the heavenly places,

v. 21, Far above all principality, and power, and might and dominion, and every name that is named not only in this world, but also in that which is to come:

v. 22, And hath put all things under his feet, and gave him to be the head over all things to the Church,

v. 23, Which is his body, the fulness of him that filleth all in all.

Praise GOD People! In this passage, we see GOD the Father, we see GOD the Son, and we see GOD the Holy Spirit. In verse three, this passage speaks of GOD blessing us with all Spiritual blessings in Christ Jesus. In verse four it speaks of all of it being planned before the foundation of the world. In various verses, it talks of Spiritual blessings and reminds us of the Eternal inheritance in verse eleven. That inheritance is for now and for Eternity. Praise GOD! The last four verses speak of Jesus being seated at the right hand of GOD and having all power far above all things for ever, "Eternally".

So you see, GOD is love, and GOD and Jesus and The Holy Spirit are one and the same. And the Bible says in HEBREWS 13:8,

v. 8, Jesus Christ the same yesterday, and today, and forever.

So in all of this, we can see that GOD The Father, and Jesus, and The Holy Spirit are the same, yesterday, and today, and forever. It is clear to see that GOD is love and that love itself is the same yesterday, and today, and forever. Love is Eternal!

Glory to GOD! Another outstanding Characteristic of Love is, The Eternality of Love....

Chapter Ten

Love, Love, Love

2 nd CORINTHIANS 13:14

The grace of the Lord Jesus Christ, and the love of God, and the Communion of the Holy Ghost, be with you all. Amen.

Hallelujah! Let me tell you when GOD gave me the title for this last Chapter, I really did not understand why HE wanted me to title it Love, Love, Love. But Praise GOD, as I diligently sat down and prayerfully wrote the first nine Chapters, GOD started slowly opening the eyes of my understanding to why HE gave me Love, Love, Love. HE gave it to me because GOD is love. HE is the ultimate picture of love, in all of it's majesty and splendor.

So since GOD is love, then it is fair, Biblical, and very GOD-inspired to say that Jesus and the Holy Spirit is also love. So when GOD gave me that title for this final Chapter, HE gave me one for the Father, one for the Son, and one for the Holy Spirit. Praise GOD!

Some people claim that the doctrine of the Trinity is false doctrine. That is downright nonsense. Even Jesus taught and spoke about the

Holy Trinity. Look at a verse where Jesus spoke of the Trinity. It is
MATTHEW 28:19, it says:

v. 19, Go ye therefore and teach all nations, baptizing them in the
name of the Father, and of the Son, and of the Holy Ghost:

People of GOD, that is just one verse of many that Jesus spoke of
the Trinity. So don't you let anyone tell you that the Trinity doctrine
is false doctrine. Jesus does not teach false doctrine my friend! And
the teaching of the Trinity does not limit GOD or put HIM in a box
as some may say. You can see the work of the Trinity all throughout
the Bible. Praise GOD! You see, just because we read in the Bible that
GOD is on the throne, and Jesus is seated on HIS throne at the right
hand of GOD does not mean that they are just sitting there twiddling
their thumbs.

I can assure you that all three are very much active in our lives
today. That is why I used my opening verse, let's look at it again, 2nd
CORINTHIANS 13:14, it says:

v. 14, The grace of the Lord Jesus Christ, and the love of God, and
the Communion of the Holy Ghost, be with you all. Amen.

So you can see here in this verse, we see a very vivid picture of the
Holy Trinity. The Father is love, The Son is love, and The Holy Spirit
is love. And all three are alive and active in every believer's life, for the
duration of our lives here on earth. You need to remember that Jesus
said in one of the Gospels, that HE and The Father had been working,
since the beginning of Creation, and we know that the Holy Spirit has
been working as well. Also in HEBREWS it says, they are the same
yesterday, today, and forever, and that goes for Father, Son, and Holy
Spirit, Past, "Present" and future. They are all three still working today
in our lives.

Please allow me to show you some Scripture that will prove my point. Look at MARK 16:15-20, it says:

v. 15, And he said unto them, Go ye into all the world, and preach the gospel to every creature.

v. 16, He that believeth and is baptized shall be saved; but he that believeth not shall be damned.

v. 17, And these signs shall follow them that believe; In my name shall they cast out devils; they shall speak with new tongues;

v. 18, They shall take up serpents; and if they drink any deadly thing, it shall not hurt them; they shall lay hands on the sick, and they shall recover.

v. 19, So then after the Lord had spoken unto them, he was received up into heaven, and sat on the right hand of God.

v. 20, And they went forth, and preached every where, the Lord working with them, and confirming the word with signs following. Amen.

Praise GOD Christian People, these very verses show very clearly that Jesus is alive and active in every believer's life. Verses 15 through 18 are speaking of everyone who believes in Jesus. Then in verse 19, you see where Jesus sat down at the right hand of GOD. When a king takes his throne, he does not just sit on it all of the time people. That just means that he took his place of authority for all Eternity.

You can see in the very last verse of this passage, that Jesus is still working in every believer's life, Look at it again, it says:

v. 20, And they went forth, and preached everywhere, the Lord working with them, and confirming the word with signs following. Amen.

So you see, "after" Jesus finished speaking, after HE was received up into heaven, and after HE sat on the right hand of GOD, it says "the Lord working with them". Jesus is very alive and active in our lives today dear people. And we have seen that Jesus Himself is love, HE is another powerful source of love alive and working in our lives forever. Praise GOD!

Let me explain to you that I am convinced that love and learning to love is a life-long experience for the believer. We are never to think too highly of ourselves or look down on anyone for how little or how much love we see in their lives. Love is a GOD given gift of the Spirit, and all three members of the Holy Trinity will be helping all believers to learn to love the way GOD wants us to love one another throughout our lives on earth.

Let me show you some verses to prove my point to you concerning the Father being alive and active in all Christians lives. Let's look at it in ROMANS 12:3, it says:

v. 3, For I say through the grace given unto me, to every man that is among you, not to think of himself more highly than he ought to think; but to think soberly, according as God hath dealt to every man the measure of faith.

My dear friend, this passage is referring to GOD the Father dealing to every man the measure of faith. You can also determine from this verse that, since GOD is love, HE will also deal to every believer a measure of love throughout the duration of his or her life on earth. So you can see very clearly that GOD the Father is also very alive and active in the believer's life today. Glory to GOD!

Now let's look at some Scripture to show that the Holy Spirit is alive and active in all believers lives. Let's look at GALATIANS 5:22-23, it says:

v. 22, But the fruit of the Spirit is love, joy, peace, longsuffering, gentleness, goodness, faith,

v. 23, Meekness, temperance: against such there is no law.

So Praise GOD! We can see here that the Holy Spirit is also very much alive and active in the believers' lives. And since these things are the fruit of the Spirit, they are also the fruit of the Father and of the Son. Fruit of the Holy Trinity! All three members of the Holy Trinity are always working to impart this fruit in every Christians life. They all three are also working to help the believer function in the gifts of the Spirit, which are also gifts of the Holy Trinity. Praise GOD!

As we look back at the fruit of the Spirit, we can see very clearly that the fruit itself is more Characteristics of Love. The Supernatural gifts of GOD are also more Characteristics of Love. There are many, many Characteristics of Love. And just as we have seen thus far in our study, The Father is Eternal, The Son, (Jesus) is Eternal, and The Holy Spirit is Eternal. My Dear Christian Friend, you can rest assured that the unfailing power of love is an Eternal force also.

Love is a force that GOD is continuously working to instill in all believers. GOD wants to instill love in us because HE knows how powerful it is. Look at these verses if you would like:

1st CORINTHIANS 13:8 says: love never fails;

EPHESIANS 5:2 says: to walk in love;

1st JOHN 4:18 says: that Perfect love casts out fear;

1st JOHN 4:7 says: whoever loves is born of God.

Fellow Christians, love is a powerful force. And we in our human nature cannot truly love one another the way GOD wants us to. That is why HE Himself imparts the ability in us to love the way HE does.

The Bible tells us to love our enemies, so we can rest assured that GOD will give us the ability to do that. When we begin to function in love the way GOD wants us to, we will be able to reach out and love the unlovable person that we never thought we could reach. We will love them right on into the body of Christ. They may be the meanest and ugliest and most hard-hearted person you have ever seen in your life. Oh, but Glory to GOD, when you start witnessing to them and showing them that you love them and that GOD loves them and wants to bless them in all areas of their life, you will see that the Bible is true.

Love never fails, and as you show love to that person, you will see the hardness just crumble. You will see that stony heart begin to turn to a heart of flesh, and you will begin to see the evil Spirits flee and the broken Spirit that GOD loves so well, shine forth. No matter how hard they may be, they cannot stand against the force of love.

As we learned earlier in our study, if we ever get to the point that we could love like Moses loved, so much that we would kill for someone or that we would even go to hell for them. There is no telling what kind of miracles GOD would do through us. Now I'm not saying that we should kill for someone, I am only saying, that if we could love someone that much. And I am not saying that we should go to hell for someone, just that we could love them that much. GOD would not allow us to do that. Just like HE did not allow Moses to. But, HE would indeed acknowledge our limitless love and HE would bless us to the point that all we could see was miracles, miracles, and more miracles of love in our everyday lives.

So you see precious people of GOD, we can look all the way back to before Creation, and we can see GOD the Father, GOD the Son, and GOD the Holy Spirit working the force of love in HIS people's lives. From GENESIS to REVELATION, we see the Holy Trinity imparting the force of love in the people of GOD'S lives. We see love working in our lives daily as we try our very best to live for GOD. And we can also look to the Word of GOD for the promises that HE will be imparting the power of love in our lives all of our days on earth. Praise GOD!

So once again let's refer to what Moses, a mighty man of GOD had to say as his life was coming to a close. Look at DEUTERONOMY 3:24, it says:

v. 24, O Lord God, thou hast begun to shew thy servant thy greatness, and thy mighty hand: for what God is there in heaven or in earth, that can do according to thy works, and according to thy might?

Glory to GOD Christian People! I am convinced that GOD will indeed be using us to shine forth HIS love to a lost and dying world, right up until the very end of our lives just like HE did with Moses. Walking in GOD'S love is a life-long experience for all Christians, and we are assured in this, that in the Father, in the Son, and in the Precious Holy Spirit, we will always find love, love, love. Hallelujah!

POWER PRAYER

For Salvation and to be baptized in the Holy Spirit.

Father GOD, I come to you as humbly as I know how. Lord, your word says in 1st JOHN 1:9, "If we confess our sins, he is faithful and just to forgive us our sins, and to cleanse us from all unrighteousness". So I confess to you that I have sinned in many ways. I now repent and turn away from my sins and I ask you to forgive me and cleanse me from all of my unrighteousness, in the name of Jesus.

Father, your word also says in ROMANS 10:9-10, "That if thou shalt confess with thy mouth the Lord Jesus, and shalt believe in thine heart that God hath raised him from the dead, thou shalt be saved. For with the heart man believeth unto righteousness; and with the mouth confession is made unto Salvation.

So I confess with my mouth that I believe Jesus died on the Cross so I can be saved and I believe with all my heart that GOD raised him from the dead and I ask you to come into my life and save me. I now accept Jesus as my Lord and Savior and I believe with all my heart that your word is true, and that I am saved by grace.

Father your word also says in the Book of LUKE 11:13, "If ye then being evil, know how to give good gifts unto your children: how much more shall your heavenly Father give the Holy Spirit to them that ask him?

So Father I ask you to give me the gift of the Holy Spirit. I ask you to fill me till my cup runs over, and allow me to successfully function in the gifts of the Spirit that are mentioned in your word. So that I will become an effective witness for Jesus and a blessing to others for the rest of my life. In Jesus' name I pray.

Amen.

If you have prayed this prayer, you can believe without a doubt that you are saved. The Bible says you shall be saved. That is a promise, and it is also a promise that GOD will fill you with the Holy Spirit, if you ask HIM. So now you need to join a good Church and sincerely turn away from your old sinful life, and walk in and enjoy the new Spirit filled life that GOD has given you. The old you should start fading into the past, and the new you will start shining brightly as you seek to serve GOD in all that you do.

www.ingramcontent.com/pod-product-compliance
Lightning Source LLC
Chambersburg PA
CBHW051329120626
46547CB00016B/2460